DESIDERIUM

A COLLECTION OF LOVE SICK POEMS

ALEXANDRIA LEE

CONTENTS

Dedicated to those hopeless souls waiting to get it right

A Note

If you've read any of my books, you know my writing
tends to veer quite poetic.

However, poetry was never anything I intended on writ-
ing. Though, as it is with most art, I wasn't given much
of a choice once inspiration hit.
For the several months I penned down these random
poems and verses, my brain felt trapped in lyrical setting
and refused to put out anything that wasn't poetry. I was
furious with my inability to move past these thoughts,
but I needed to get them out or they'd drive me mad.
That's the kind of obsessive passion that's fueled every
book I've written so far, so I decided to let my brain have
this detour creative outlet—I'm so relieved I did.

These poems are my love letter to the experience of
letting go.

Of expectations we trap ourselves in.
Of fears that dictate our choices.
Of people we aren't meant to love, now or maybe ever.

Dead Flowers

Maybe I was morbid, but I liked dead flowers
Because they reminded me of us
The prospect of something vibrant and breathtaking
But the timing wasn't right
We didn't have enough time in the sun
Or rainfall to sow our roots into this earth
So, consequently, we died like flowers do—and I found
that comforting
Because souls like flowers don't truly perish
They keep getting reborn from tiny seeds left behind
Trying harder in the next life to get it right

That's what we'd do too
Keep dying just to keep trying

Hoping one day our roots take
And we find out that fulfillment tastes like sunlight and
dreams

Smoke

You have a touch that lingers like *smoke*
The scent of you sticking to my clothes for days
Your hand on my waist leaving an imprint of heat for too
many hours, searing my sensibilities to ash
Your skin, a balm and torture like all best addictions
One graze, and my pores infuse with the heady hit
Sweltering, gasping, *blazing* for more
And I'd sooner rather be set on fire and burned alive in
my vices

Than freeze to death without knowing a touch like yours

Last night, I saw you
And the night before that too
You crept inside my head
Made yourself at home in my bed
Beneath the sheets
Against the wall
Just the start of the insanity we'd befall
Because last night, you saw me too
I came to you from out of the blue
A lovely vision of frustration
For which we'd search months for an explanation
Again and again it would happen, you see
This late night awakening between you and me
Mouths used

Souls wrought
Convincing us of this thing we were not
Maybe something we were
Maybe something we will be
For now, inspiring only conscious agony
Foreshadows or lovesick memories
These teasing, taunting fantasies
Mad I will surely go
As I fear we will never know
Presently, only one thing is true
That tonight...

I can't wait to see you

Our Duet

I wondered what was so familiar about you
Until I finally heard it

Until I heard your heart in the silence and realized
It beat to the same peculiar rhythm as mine

And as I lay in bed, I wondered what thoughts lulled him
to sleep.
Mostly, I wondered if they were about me.
Did I haunt his thoughts like he haunted mine?
Was I a frustration he couldn't block out?
Head against his pillow, did he ever wish I was there,
Warming the skin right above his heart with quiet
breathing and whispered nothings,
A strong hand tangled in my hair and the other on my
unclothed back,
Stroking in unhurried lines while my fingers drew hid-
den messages on his chest.
And if the answer was yes,
Then I had to know.

Did he regard my enduring ghost as heavenly
Or hellacious
Or something in between

8

Just like us?

Drowning

I am drowning in thoughts of you

Gasping for relief in the pockets of time when my mind
forgets you exist

Paper Truths

Whenever it gets too much, I have to write you out of
my head
Bleed you onto the page so I can touch you
Run my fingers over thoughts of you I can't escape
Feel the ache of you against my skin
Dirty, Pretty, Poisoned words
Just like
Filthy, Lovely, Lethal us

Sixth Sense

I miss you to a distracting degree
Unable to think without the sting of your presence in my
thoughts,
Feeling a hollow ache cave in my chest as soon as you
leave a room.
When did this happen?
When did you get so deep?
You're a poison injected directly into my bloodstream,
Corrupting my nerve endings to obsess
Over your skin on mine
Your graveled voice in my ear
The gasps and groans we'd give and take.
Your toxins rewired my brain to picture you
Around every corner

Inside every room
Waiting for me like I wait for you.
When did the scent of the cedar-crisp breeze trigger
reminders
Of your crooked smile
Your screaming eyes
All the best and loudest parts of you?
Your venom melted on my tongue so bittersweet,
Tasting of sour apples
Of dark chocolate
Of us.
The infection of you bore an awareness so razor sharp
against my mind,
I'm positive if someone cracked my head open,
They'd find your name carved with love on the inside.

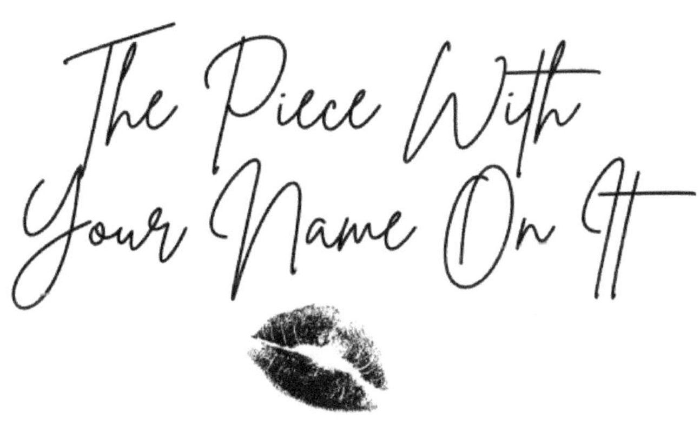

The Piece With Your Name On It

Do you think it's possible to fall in love just a little bit?
Not with your whole heart
But rather just a piece of it?
I do, I think
It's what makes sense
Or else why is your name written on my soul in ink?
It's bled through the fabric of my being
Stained my thoughts so I see you even when I'm sleeping
Overrunning my dreams
Shredding my morals at the seams
Though, for all of this said
And how often you take up residence inside my head
I don't want all of you, you see
Just the part that belongs to me

You know the one
You have one too
It's that tiny part of me that belongs to you

14

Your Eyes Talk

When you look at me
You don't do it with your eyes
But with your soul
And I feel it *everywhere*
Like a feather made of fire
Soft and scorching
Melting through flesh and bones
Searing through to my bare and blistered heart
Holding the naked thing
Bringing your lips to it
Awakening it with a whisper—

"I found you"

She wrote him cryptic poetry
He gave her dead flowers
They spoke through their silence
Composing 'what-ifs'
And finding each other during the night hours

She liked his winter gaze
He loved her candied scent
Two mirrored and wretched souls
For whom time
Refused to relent

It ravaged their potential
Threw gasoline on a fire with nowhere left to spread

Mouths cold
Bodies still
Always wondering where it might have led

They liked it that way though
Romanticizing their crossed fates
Hiding their affections in the safety of 'never'
Masochistic hearts

Unlikely, unbidden soulmates

Pretty Little Lies

♡

"Love is all you need" is my least favorite lie

Love is simple
It's a symptom of being alive
A consequence of fate
People fall in love without meaning to because love is
just that opportunistic

You and I weren't looking
We walked right into it and were blindsided by the crash
Love knocked into us so hard
It concussed our hearts
Making them forget that we couldn't have each other

Not now
Not in this life

Because love is *not* all you need

Timing is the sadistic necessity
And time was not on our side

It never had been

You, Wretched You

I burn and I ache and I miss

All sensations I yearn to dismiss

Back to basics

Back to before

Back to when I had no idea it was you I was looking for

We were constellations written out of our reach
Meant to meet
Meant to fall
Meant to crash
Our destiny was destruction and implosion
And all we could do was brace ourselves

Silence is the love language of the

Damned and Star-Crossed

We'd Ruin It

In all the strange ways we align
I never once wanted you to be mine

That would have ruined it, you see
This little world we built just you and me

We were safe in our dreams
Hearts steady at the seams

There was nothing to risk
Because what you and I had did not exist

Not in touch, Not in words
Nothing but two silent songbirds

You could hear me, and I could hear you
But that's as far as our melody grew

It was quite perfect that way
Solidifying it to this very day

An untouchable, unblemished affinity
That will stretch on into infinity

Almost

Perhaps my destiny is in 'Almost'

Almost chosen
Almost loved
Almost enough

Perhaps, I was meant to taste happiness but never swallow it

I hold it on my tongue, waiting with blind and eager patience, never noticing it diluting until it makes me sick

Perhaps, my fate is to live on the brink of starvation
And, perhaps, that is okay

I'll live in the space between life and death
Where I am
Almost beautiful enough
Almost the one
Almost worth an unbroken promise

In this limbo, I will smile and laugh and live in my day-
dreams

Where my stomach is full
The taste of love doesn't end in sickness
And I am not *Happily Ever Almost*

I would write our love story

But it doesn't have a happy ending

Purgatory

We are a stifled gasp for breath, you and I
The urge for life on the tips of our tongues
But our lungs squeeze
Teeth gnash
Oxygen stales
Sitting still and trapped in the limbo of relief
Suffocating. Dying. Waiting.

Always and eternally waiting

We'll Get it Right

If you're the moon and I'm the rose, then everything they taught me about photosynthesis in school is utter bullshit.

The sun is what feeds the flowers, but you're what feeds me.

Maybe it's parasitic. Maybe it's unhealthy.

But what you and I have is what breathes life into me.

You said that we're both made of darkness, and that's why we see the little bit of light in each other, but what if it's not light—but diamonds?

What if we aren't seeing the light that's lasted but the indestructible beauty that built inside us both?

Diamonds are formed after unbelievable pressure, and so were we.

I like to think that we're both hiding diamonds in our souls, and you can see mine and I can see yours because our broken pieces reflect off of each other.

Maybe that's why I feel you like you're a part of me.

Maybe that's why we're star-crossed.

But the thing about being star-crossed is that we have infinite galaxies to get it right, don't we? We're the stuff of forever.

You and I are forever.

Blissfully Blind

Better to be blind for eternity
Than glimpse the love of your life
And live an eternity without them

Blake

To be loved by him was an experience of masochism I
never knew I'd crave

Meet Me Among the Stars

Somewhere between the sunset and sunrise
I will find you

Peace is Overrated

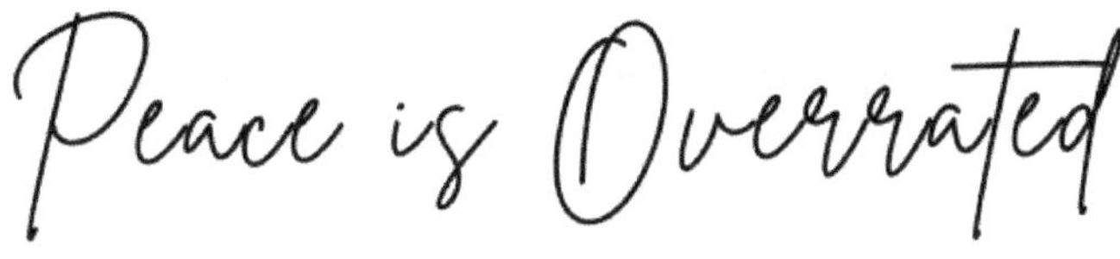

I'm healed, I said
All better, I smiled

Then you came along
And proved me all wrong

Feelings Are Nonconsensual

Don't blame me for your feelings
For your guilt
Your transgressions

All I did was exist.
Your heart did the rest.

I didn't cause them on purpose.
I didn't spell your heart with affections

So don't make me the villain
Just to ease the burden of your imperfections

Sometimes I wish I weren't a romantic
Following my raw heart blindly
Unable to convince myself to settle for less than what
the cosmos designed for my wayward soul

I wish I were logical in love
Accepting what was smart and stable and perfectly fine
Rather than holding out for a heroin chemistry and
those revered sparks of fate

It would be easier that way, wouldn't it?
To not need to have my heart moved and swept away
like ocean waves caught in the wind's riptide

Or feel the compass between my ribs spin out in a burst
of ecstasy when it finally feels the pull in the direction
of home

These sensations live in me like shadows, like memories
I haven't made yet or don't recall
They haunt and compel me
Destroy and revive me

My love, a cursed and blessed thing

My creed

My undoing

I Make Myself Sick

I've loved bad men
Narcissistic to the core.
I spent my days picking apart
Their rot-soaked layers
Loving their bruises
Feeding parts of myself to the voracious parasites living inside
Soaking these men in sunshine and redemption.
I've filled myself with their toxic nourishment
Smiling through the nausea and pain.
And yet when the day is done
It is them,
Those bad and wicked men,
Who leave me

Sick and weakened from trying to sustain their love.

The Saltwater Beast

Hate and love were like swimming, except one hap-
pened in a pool and one happened in the ocean.
One, you could swim around without worry, open your
eyes under the water, and touch the bottom if you got
tired.
The water was calm and non-threatening.
That was hate.

Love was the ocean.

It was unpredictable, creating waves to roll you up in,
only to crash you back down in a tumble of salt watery
eyes and burning lungs.

It was infested with vicious animals, lurking and waiting
to attack if you didn't drown in the riptides first.
One way or another, the ocean would destroy you, and
love was marked with that same promise.

That Pretty Ugly Thing

You know those weeds that look like flowers?
I think that might be me.
A subjective beauty with a soul of poison;
Get too close and you'll see.
My exterior, a clever disguise,
Flushed petals. Dainty leaves. Sweet exposition.
Onlookers gaze and grope without permission.
With greedy fingers, they pluck me free,
Shredding my roots, holding me too tight,
So sure the one they want is me.
They take and plant my loose ends in their lives,
Eager to show off their pretty little prize.
Poor souls, don't they know?
In me, only pain and sickness grows.

Soon, my roots stretch deep and the infection begins to
seep.
The perfect life around me wilts and chokes,
Suffocating on my wickedness that runs soul deep.
To their garden, I lay ruin
As they turn to me and shout, "What went wrong?"
As if it's my fault.
As if they've despised me all along.
In return, I want to say, weep, *plead*,
That it wasn't all me.
That if they'd looked at me closer from the start,

They'd have noticed my withered and troubled little
heart.

An Ocean's Worth of Tears

Eyes dry
Nose raw
Heart cracked

bleeding, bleeding, bleeding

When You Leave Me Alone Too Long

It is an unexpectedly cruel encounter with grief to real-
ize the great loves you've experienced weren't all that
great

The mind is simply an exceptional trickster and the
heart an easy fool

The Paradox of Us

I find myself halfway drunk with relief that our abstract
chaos is at its end
And at the same time unable to catch my breath beneath
all this fucking sadness

Forget-Me-Not

I want to say when it's done, it's done
But an unsmotherable part of me knows that's a lie;
Our souls will never be finished with each other

Sometimes I wonder if it was it all in our heads,
A twelve-tiered cake made out of crumbs.
Two hopeless hearts high off a whiff of sweetened
dreams,
Imagining delusions of destiny to fill their empty stom-
achs,
Getting drunk off small sips of affection,
Filling in the blackouts with blurry tales of fate and
meant-to-bes.
There was always that chance.
That we'd made it all up.
And though true as that was, it was just as possible we
didn't.
That it was real.

That it was real and weird and perfect and doomed and
true
Me and you.
Maybe we found each other across the stars.
Maybe we let a spark of chemistry blow us out of pro-
portion.
Maybe, I think
It's really not all that important.
The cynic and romantic in me both tend to agree,
The *how* is inconsequential when the *what* is as inex-
plicable as we.

It Happened to Me

It happened to me
That thing I write about
That all-consuming addiction to another soul
The kind that feels etched into the stars and deliciously
ruinous
The kind that feels like rain hitting the ground
Inevitable and explosive
The kind that starves your sense of sanity
The kind that is honest to fuck impossible to explain
because it sort of feels like magic

The kind that you can't have

The kind that was over before it began

The kind that's like a fire forced to exist without oxygen
Suffocating and hopeless
The kind that inflicts the burden on two people of
knowing they could fall in love with someone else if the
circumstances were right
The kind that lingers and loudens when the night is quiet
and still
It happened to me
It happened to us

Maybe one day I'll write about it

Goodbyes Are For Lovers

And because we were never real
I get to make up our happily never after
Filled with tearful admissions
Hands that know no restrictions
Confessions we'd screamed with our eyes
Finally escape our nearing lips
You hold me and I cling to you
I say how I hate goodbyes with tears wetting my cheeks
You thumb them all away while saying you know
And that this isn't goodbye
You'll find me again
Someday, somehow, some life after this
I ask if it was real or all in our heads
Your browline furrows and you rest it against mine

Whispering softly what we both already knew
You think to pull away, back to safety, back to that place
where you and I don't exist
Instead you give in this once and place your lips between
mine for the first and final time
Holding us there, in that space where it's all okay
In that limbo only we can explain
The one that tastes like candied flowers and relief and
someday
A whimper slips through, feeding you the ache that's
been burning in my chest for months that finally feels
relief
Your fingers savoring their time around my waist tighten
because *you know*
You're sorry and I'm sorry
For letting it happen, for letting it not
We wrap ourselves up in each other for a few moments
more
Trying not to notice how instinctual it all is
How naturally our hands roam and mouths pull, as if
they'd been born to do just that
How a kiss has never dipped deeper into our souls and
held on for dear life
How painful the parting will be when it comes
And then it does, that dreadful, terrible parting
We pull away slowly, ripping ourselves apart like stitches
giving way
And we breathe
And we stay still

And we internalize the pain but don't pretend it's not
there because we've done enough of that
In our locked eyes, we speak as we've always done and
say that thing we both know
That thing we both hate
Say *I'd love you if I could but we have to wait*

I'll never know why this thing woke up when it did
Why it waited so long or what to do with it now that
you're gone
It'll sit inside me like an ache I can't cure, hurting and
hoping for one day more
All I do know is this:
When that one day comes, months, years, lifetimes from
now
And you find me in the street, in the park, dancing alone
in the starry dark
My eyes, my hair, and even my heart will all be new
But still I'll find myself stopping and staring at you
Because no matter the time
No matter the distance
Love,
My soul will always remember you

Thank you for reading!

If you enjoyed these forbidden love poems and haven't read any of Alexandria's books, find her Amazon to dive into the rest of her angsty romance catalogue: https://www.amazon.com/stores/author/B08PQ3F8LB

The poems *Constellations, We'll Get It Right,* and *The Saltwater Beast* are from her best-selling trilogy, the *Star-Crossed Series*, available on Amazon and Kindle Unlimited.